Ways to Be Smart About
Money

Rebecca Vickers

www.raintreepublishers.co.uk
Visit our website to find out
more information about
Raintree books.

To order:
☎ Phone 0845 6044371
🖹 Fax +44 (0) 1865 312263
💻 Email myorders@raintreepublishers.co.uk

Customers from outside the UK please telephone +44 1865 312262

Raintree is an imprint of Capstone Global Library
Limited, a company incorporated in England and Wales
having its registered office at 7 Pilgrim Street, London,
EC4V 6LB – Registered company number: 6695582

Text © Capstone Global Library Limited 2011
First published in hardback in 2011
Paperback edition first published in 2012
The moral rights of the proprietor have been asserted.

Edited by Andrew Farrow and Vaarunika Dharmapala
Designed by Richard Parker
Picture research by Ruth Blair
Originated by Capstone Global Library Ltd
Printed and bound in China by South China Printing
  Company Ltd

ISBN 978 1 406 21745 2 (hardback)
15 14 13 12 11
10 9 8 7 6 5 4 3 2 1

ISBN 978 1 406 21771 1 (paperback)
16 15 14 13 12
10 9 8 7 6 5 4 3 2 1

British Library Cataloguing in Publication Data
Vickers, Rebecca.
101 ways to be smart about money.
332'.024-dc22
A full catalogue record for this book is available
from the British Library.

Acknowledgments
We would like to thank the following for permission to
reproduce photographs: Alamy p **43** (Ei Katsumata);
Nora Coon p **6**; Corbis pp **13** (Gary I Rothstein/epa), **14**
(Jamie Grill/Tetra Images), **32** (Tyrone Turner/National
Geographic Society); iStockphoto pp **9** (Chris Price), **15**
(Jason Stitt), **20** (Bob Ingelhart), **29** (Mayumi Terao),
41 (Jen Grantham); Photolibrary pp **24** (TAO Images
Limited); Shutterstock pp **4** (Andresr), **5** (Nousha), **7**
(Alexander Kalina), **18** (Valentyn Volkov), **19** (Nemida),
21 (Clara), **22** (Robyn Mackenzie), **23** (Thinglass), **27**
(Yuri Arcurs), **28** (CandyBoxPhoto), **31** (Denis Pepin),
34 (Worytko Pawel), **35** (haveseen), **36** (cozyta), **37**
(Wire_man), **39** (Yuri Arcurs), **45** (prism68), **47** (Greg
Perkins), **48** (Chavdar), **50** (PhotoSky 4t com).

Cover photograph of a pile of coins, reproduced with
permission of iStockphoto (ooyoo).

Every effort has been made to contact copyright holders
of material reproduced in this book. Any omissions will
be rectified in subsequent printings if notice is given to
the publisher.

Disclaimer

Contents

In order to protect the privacy of individuals featured in case studies, some names have been changed.

Words appearing in the text in bold, **like this**, are explained in the Glossary.

Are you money smart?

Money is a big part of your life. It's great to get a chance to earn your own money and decide how you want to use it. By being money smart you can get the best out of your hard work and get good value from your spending and saving. Go for it!

Many things that you want will cost you money. Just make sure you get good value for your cash.

01 Put all your loose small change into a jar or bowl. Don't lose it in the wash, down the back of sofas, or in the back of drawers. You'll find that the jar soon fills up and adds up!

02 When you go shopping, make a list of the things you really need. That way you're less likely to spend money on things you don't need.

03 Think twice before ordering soft drinks in cafés and restaurants. The cost is high for what you get. Remember, tap water is free.

04 When you're planning to get something expensive, such as an MP3 player, don't rush into buying the first one you like. Do some online research to check and compare prices. You'll be surprised at how much you might save.

Quiz

Are you a money dummy?

1) You are given money for your birthday. Do you:
   a. use it as part of your usual spending money
   b. go out and buy an item that you've wanted for ages
   c. put it in a savings account?

2) When you go out for the day, do you:
   a. take all the cash you have with you in case you need it
   b. think about what you are planning to do and take enough money to cover your expenditure
   c. take no cash so you don't buy things you don't need?

3) It's safer to put your money in your pocket than to keep it in a purse or bag.
   a. true
   b. false
   c. both can be risky.

Each coin may be worth very little, but together it all adds up.

Nora Coon: writing her way to success

When she was only 12 years old, American schoolgirl Nora Coon pitched an idea for a book to a publisher's representative at a writing convention. By the time she was 17, 3 of her non-fiction books for teens had been published. And by 22, she was an established writer. How did she make this happen?

Nora knew that her talents were storytelling and writing, and decided early to make her dream of being a writer come true. Her second book, *Teen Dream Jobs*, was written to help other teens find the careers they want. Nora has not let her diabetes and epilepsy hold her back. In fact, one of her books, *The Diabetes Game*, focuses on young people with this disease. Nora has made her talents, knowledge, and personal experiences really work for her.

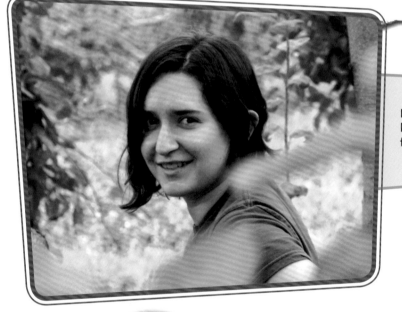

Nora Coon didn't let anything stop her fulfilling her dreams.

"All teenagers are stupid about money. It's just a phase you have to go through."

Do you agree with this 15-year-old's opinion? Do you think Nora Coon would agree?

Don't despair! There are many ways to go about earning some spending money.

Aim for the top!

05 Good ideas and money-making schemes can come to you whatever your age. Be confident, and who knows where your ideas could lead!

06 Remember, your own talents and experiences are key to your financial success. Being clever about how you use your money is as important as how you make it.

07 If there are things you want but can't afford, consider making them yourself.

08 If fears and excuses are holding you back in life, then be brave and get on with things!

09 Make firm money plans and stick to them. This is the start of being money smart.

It all adds up

The fact is you can't save or spend money if you haven't got any! So, how do you get hold of some hard cash? You usually start by getting pocket money from your parents, possibly for household jobs you do, and as presents at birthdays and Christmas.

Negotiating your pocket money

In the adult world, salary negotiations can be difficult and complicated. Coming to an agreement with your parents over your pocket money can be just as difficult! If you bear in mind the following tips, you'll have a firm and fair base to start your bargaining.

10 Work out which of your expenses your pocket money will cover. Will it include school lunches and clothes, or will it also pay for things such as school trips and extra activities? Make a list of all the household jobs that you're expected to do in order to get your pocket money.

11 Do you feel you need extra pocket money to deal with rising costs or unexpected additional expenses? Write out a clear list of these to show your parents. But remember, if your parents say a firm NO, you need to accept that the negotiations are over.

12 Your negotiations will be more successful if you can be trusted to be sensible. If you are careless or stupid with your money, you can't expect your parents to be sympathetic to requests for more.

BE SMART

Everyone's different
Remember that the work schedules and finances of every family are different. A fair agreement with your parents might not be anything like the arrangements your friends have.

If you do a really good job of cleaning someone's car, they may ask you to do it again or recommend you to others.

"I made my allowance as a kid cleaning toilets. I'm actually pretty good at it."

Jennifer Aniston, actor

Earning money

The pocket money you get from your parents will never seem like quite enough! So, what do you do?

There are lots of ways you can earn money by helping others out, for example, babysitting, car-washing, or gardening. You also need to think about how much time you have and if you will have to spend any money for equipment. Relatives, friends, and neighbours can be good customers. However, if you are looking further afield, you'll need to advertise yourself.

So, how do I market "me"?

If you want customers other than your relatives and friends, there are ways to market yourself without spending big money. Simple, clear information is all that's needed.

13 Make your own business cards on a computer by printing your details on to thin cardboard and cutting them out. A business card should give your name, contact details, and clearly state the work you can do. A memorable or interesting business name, such as "Matt and his Mower", can give you an edge over the competition.

14 Use a computer to design a flier or poster to advertise your services. There are notice boards in many places that let you put up small posters for free or for a small charge. It won't cost you anything except a bit of your time to hand-deliver posters and fliers to houses in your neighbourhood.

15 When you have done a job for someone, ask if they would be happy to recommend you to others. A personal recommendation from a satisfied customer is the best free advertising.

16 The most important tip for anyone running their own business, even if it is just mowing grass or babysitting, is that THE CUSTOMER IS ALWAYS RIGHT. They are paying you, so if they don't want their kids to watch television, or want their grass cuttings put in bin bags, as long as it's legal, give them what they want.

A bit of work and imagination on your part can help attract customers.

Happy Dogs

Pet Care and Walking Service

Local recommendations available

Jenny Kendall
barkingmad97@zedmail.com

The world of work

As you get older, you and your friends will eventually get part-time, weekend, or holiday jobs. Remember: you ARE protected! Most countries have rules about the age you have to be before you can work, the maximum numbers of hours you can work in a week, and the minimum amount of pay per hour that you can earn. So when the time is right, just how do you get the job?

17 Think about the kind of place you would like to work in. It's true that most people eventually get part-time jobs in shops and restaurants, but why not try something different? If you've always wanted to work with animals, ask your local vet's practice or pet shop if they have any part-time or Saturday work.

18 Prepare a simple **curriculum vitae** (CV) to give out. If you want to get a good job that pays well, you need to present yourself well. You will stand out from other applicants if you have a well laid out CV with all your contact details.

What's that?
Curriculum vitae are Latin words meaning "the course of life". The initials CV are often used as a short form. A CV is a brief report of a person's education and work experience, as well as certain biographical details.

Q What is **financial literacy**?

A Literacy is the ability to read and understand written words. In the same way, financial literacy means having an understanding of money and making good decisions about how to save and spend it.

When you apply for any kind of job, remember that *you* are the product you are trying to sell. To get the money, you need to get the job!

19 First impressions count! When you go for a job interview, remember how important it is to look clean, tidy, and appropriately dressed.

20 When you enquire about a job on the phone, the way you sound can influence your success. Speak clearly, politely, and give sensible answers. It may make the difference between getting a job or not.

21 Practice makes perfect. Think of the kinds of questions you might be asked on the phone or at an interview, and practise your responses beforehand.

22 When you get a job, the same behaviour that helped you to get it can make you a good employee *and* make you extra money. For example, if you are a waiter in a restaurant, being polite, helpful, and efficient can get you bigger tips from your customers.

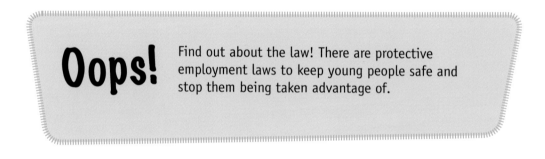

Oops!
Find out about the law! There are protective employment laws to keep young people safe and stop them being taken advantage of.

23 Don't accept any job from an employer who tries to pay you less than the minimum wage. This is the lowest amount of money by law that you can be paid per hour to do a job.

24 Never accept a job that requires you to accept "cash in hand". This probably means your employment is not official, and is therefore illegal.

25 Don't do anything you know to be dangerous, or perform tasks without the correct clothing or equipment. No amount of money is worth the risk of injuring yourself.

The teenager who sold records from the boot of his car

Today, Richard Branson and the Virgin company name are well known all over the world. But his life as an international **entrepreneur** really kicked off at the age of 16 when he produced a magazine for students.

At the age of 19, he was selling cut-price vinyl record singles from the boot of his car, and then by mail order. Within only three years of starting his first businesses, he had record shops in central London and a recording studio in the countryside. Over 40 years later, he is now one of the world's billionaires. Branson is still enlarging his business empire, and using some of his wealth to indulge his adventurous spirit with record attempts in fast boats and hot-air balloons.

Cash from a clear out

Everyone ends up with things they don't want and don't need. You grow out of clothes, and your likes and dislikes can change, too. All that extra stuff takes up space – and it can be worth money! So how can you make some cash and get that embarrassing plastic pedal car out of the garage?

26 Make sure that everything you want to sell is clean, workable, and well-presented. Wash, iron, and fold clothes and put similar sizes or types of items together. Clean up old toys and make sure all the parts of games and puzzles are in the bag or box. Make each thing look like it is worth buying.

27 Collect up all the stuff you want to sell and have a garage sale.

28 Keep an eye open for local car boot sales, but remember that you'll need transport and may have to pay a fee to take part.

29 Find local shops that let you display small postcard ads. These may be free or cost a small weekly rate.

30 Look through the local newspapers, including any free papers. There are usually sections for small "for sale" ads.

31 Identify potential customers. If you've outgrown your bike, would your friend's younger sister like it?

Even when you no longer want something, someone out there will be willing to pay you for it.

Often the best thing to do with stuff you don't need or want is to give it away to friends, relatives, or to a charity shop. Or you could have a sale for a charity. People are usually generous when buying things at a charity sale, and the cash you make can go to your chosen good cause.

If you sell an item that is jointly owned, don't forget to share out the cash.

32 Be sure that an item is yours to sell! If your parents bought you an expensive bike, you need to ask if they are happy about you selling it, or whether they want some of the money you make. If it's something that once belonged to a grandparent, it's probably not yours to sell. You might find in years to come that you're very glad you kept it!

33 When an item is jointly owned by the family, such as a garden slide, you need to agree how the money will be split before you sell it.

34 If you are selling items from an ad that gives your home phone number, check first that this is okay with your family. Then make sure that they have all of the details about the item in case you're not there when potential buyers call.

35 NEVER let anyone come to your home to pay for or pick up an item unless there are adults in the house. Have the item ready by the door, and only accept payment in cash.

When the piggybank is full...

So, your piggybank is bursting with all the cash you've saved up. Where should you keep it? You could opt for a shoebox under the bed. Or you could take the leap and enter the real money world of banks and building societies.

But is this as scary and incomprehensible as it first seems? Even more importantly, is your money really safe once you no longer have it in your hands?

listen up!

The media is full of phrases such as "credit crunch", "recession", and "low **interest** rates". It can seem really scary out there! But starting a bank or building society account is still a good idea for four main reasons:

1. Putting your money in a bank account protects it from theft, loss, or damage.
2. A bank account helps you to develop a **credit history**. If you keep to the rules, you may be able to borrow money from the bank in the future, for a **mortgage** or a business loan.
3. A bank account can get you into the habit of saving.
4. Money in savings accounts can earn you interest.

What's that?

Interest is the amount of money you get paid by a bank or building society on savings, or charged on borrowings or debt. The interest rate is the percentage paid or charged.

Good bank? Bad bank?

It's worth spending time choosing a bank or building society that will give you the best services and interest rates.

36 Do your research before choosing a bank. Make sure whichever one you choose has the right account or accounts for you. Check if there are special accounts for young people or students.

37 Try to choose a bank that does not charge fees for transactions or services provided. These charges can quickly add up.

38 Choose a bank that's convenient to get to. If the nearest branch is far away, maybe it's not for you.

39 Make sure that the bank is part of a company protected by national government guarantees. This means that any money you have in your bank account will be safe even if the bank runs into trouble.

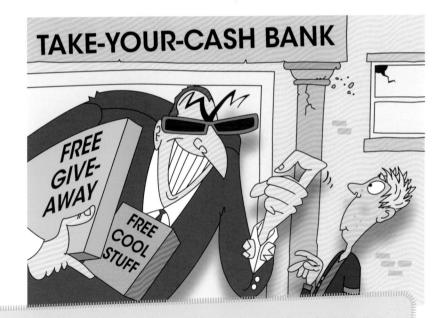

Oops! Don't be tricked by special offers or gifts that are trying to encourage you to open an account in a particular bank or building society. Always judge a bank on bank-related matters, such as interest rates and other services.

Is interest interesting?

Most banks and building societies offer a choice of different kinds of accounts. Savings accounts pay you interest to keep money in the account, rather than spend it. The amount of interest you get is based on a percentage of the amount saved. The interest is then added to the savings. This is called compounding. Look for savings accounts that give a good rate of interest and compound the interest often.

Bank cards: understanding the plastic fantastic

Credit cards, debit cards, personal identification numbers... When you get a bank account you need to learn a whole new language! You also need new knowledge and new habits.

Q What's the difference between a credit card and a debit card?

A A credit card lets you buy items and then pay at the end of the month. It is called a credit card because the company is giving you credit to buy the items.

A debit card is issued with your bank account and is used to get cash from automatic teller machines (ATMs) or to pay for items in shops. It takes money directly out of your bank account as you use it. You have to have the money in order to spend it!

Both types of cards use Chip and PIN technology. This means they have a computer chip embedded in them. You have to enter your personal identification number (PIN) before the chip will let the payment go through.

As well as credit and debit cards, you can also get prepaid credit cards. These cards work like prepaid mobile phones. You pay to have credit put on the card and then it can be used to buy things. These can be useful when you don't want to carry cash, or want to buy items on the internet or by mail order without having to give your bank details.

Oops!

Amanda thought it would be easier to remember her PIN number if she used her birth date, 10 December – or 1012. Then she had her purse stolen from her bag in a restaurant. It contained her provisional driving license, which showed her date of birth.

By the time she'd reported the theft, her card had been used at an ATM with the correct PIN! What had seemed an easy way for her to remember her PIN was also an easy guess for the thief. Choose a friend's birthday to make it harder!

Protect your information by always using one hand to cover the other when entering your PIN at an ATM or a Chip and PIN machine.

Don't throw your money around!

Cash and cards are valuable possessions. Treating them properly is an important part of being money smart.

40 Never carry more cash than you need. It can make you a target for theft and tempt you to spend more than you should.

41 Keep your cards safe! Find a secure place at home to keep debit or credit cards. If cards get stolen or lost, call the phone number relating to loss or theft on your bill or bank statement. Your card will then be deactivated so it cannot be used.

42 Never take your cards or excess cash to school. You won't need these things during the day, and they could get lost or stolen.

43 When you go out, keep cards and cash secure in your purse or wallet and carefully replace them after use.

44 Handbags containing valuables such as cash, cards, and mobile phones should be zipped up or securely fastened. Keep wallets in deep, preferably front, trouser pockets.

45 Try not to put wallets or purses in the outside pockets of your backpack. They will be safer shoved to the bottom of the largest section with other things on top.

listen up!

It can sometimes be difficult to find a secure place to keep cash or cards. This may especially be the case when you are travelling.

Experienced travellers know that hidden money belts work best. These can go around your waist and under your clothes like a belt, or around your neck inside your shirt, or they can be clipped to a bra.

Oops!

When you've just used an ATM to withdraw cash, try not to get distracted by your friends or the queue behind you. Make sure you take both your card and your cash, and put them safely away BEFORE you turn around. Make life hard for pickpockets and purse-snatchers!

BE SMART

It's best to keep valuable items in your front pockets. But in crowded places like gigs, someone may even try to reach into these. You can close up front pockets using large safety pins or nappy pins, or by sewing Velcro fastenings inside the top edges of your pockets. Or you could wear clothes with deep pockets that zip or button up.

46 In an emergency, some folded paper money can go in your shoe under your foot until you need it. It may get smelly, but it will definitely be safe!

47 For days at the beach, you can buy small, watertight containers for your money and valuables. You can wear one on a neck cord or fastened to your wrist or swimming costume.

Oops!

Money and plastic cards are not indestructible. Try to keep them safe and take good care of them. If accidents do happen, here are some ways to sort them out:

48 Oops! Your paper money has accidentally gone through the washing machine! If you're lucky, you'll just end up with really clean money. If you're unlucky, you end up with money mush. Let it dry out thoroughly and then take it to a bank. If over half of the note is there you will be able to get a replacement.

49 If money is ripped or torn up you can tape it together and still use it. However, banks will replace damaged money so long as the serial numbers on both halves match.

50 When credit cards and debit cards get scraped, bent, or cracked, or their magnetic strips get demagnetized, they may not work in ATMs or Chip and PIN machines. You'll need to contact your card provider and apply for a replacement card.

Australian dollars are made of an almost indestructible plastic material. The notes stay clean, are hard to **counterfeit**, and are recyclable!

Two words you never want to hear: fraudulent usage

Kamal was a bit shocked when his bank statement showed that he had bought over £50 of petrol at three different places in the same week. Since Kamal isn't old enough to drive and doesn't have a car he knew that something was very wrong!

Kamal immediately called the bank's customer service number on the back of his statement. He found out that he'd been the victim of **fraudulent usage** and it was probable that his debit card had been **cloned**. It took nearly a month for the bank to credit the illegally obtained money back to his account. But it could have been worse. What if he hadn't checked his bank statement?

	Money in	Money out	£ Balance
			77.38
		17.97	70.58
		6.80	50.58
		20.00	
			40.79
		9.79	20.79
		20.00	

Always check your bank statements to make sure the amounts of money going in and out of your account are correct.

Is it safe to spend?

When you've done your earning and your banking, what about a bit of spending? You deserve it! But remember, even though it's okay to spend, it isn't okay to go crazy. You need to think about the difference between needing something and wanting it, as well as about being a savvy saver.

Earning and saving your own money gives you the chance to get some of those special items you want. If you do this, you don't need to wait for birthday money or depend on the Bank of Mum and Dad!

Budgeting: keeping track of that cash

Before you can spend, you need to know how much money you have. The only way you can do that is to always keep track of your cash. As well as checking your bank statements, it's a good idea to do a simple budget. A budget sets out what you think you will spend over a weekly or monthly period. When making a budget there are a few things to remember:

51 Always be realistic when setting your budget. If you always spend a certain amount for lunch at school, don't presume you can suddenly start spending half that amount.

52 A good budget should NEVER include more outgoings (expenditure) than money you have available to spend. A budget should always balance (money in and money out should be the same). Aim to have something left at the end of the period covered by your budget.

53 Money you add to your savings should be one of the "expenditures" in your budget.

You can be your own **accountant** and your budget can be as simple or complicated as you want.

DATE	IN	OUT
25 December	£100 (Xmas money)	
1 January	£80 (January allowance)	
5 January		£65 (tickets for gig)
12 January	£12 (car cleaning)	
19 January	£15 (babysitting)	
20 January		£27 (school stuff)
23 January		£48 (shirt + shoes + DVD)
27 January		£8 (birthday present for Tom)
TOTAL FOR MONTH	£207	£148

listen up!

Make sure that when you buy something it is because you really want it, not because you have been influenced by advertising or marketing.

54 Just because something is marketed using well-known celebrities, that doesn't mean it's better, only that the company has a large advertising budget! A great jingle or catchphrase may be fun, but it doesn't make a shampoo or a deodorant more effective. Look on the internet or in specialist magazines for product reviews to get the real story of what's good and what's not.

55 Beware of the use of "placement" advertising. Companies make sure that items they want to sell to teenagers are advertised during television programmes aimed at young people. This just means that the advertisers are clever, not that the product is the best you can get.

Don't let the logo bullies get you!

Now that you know how to really look at a product and not just at who's doing the advertising, you also need to be sure that companies aren't pressuring you to part with your money in other ways.

Q What is a logo?

A A logo is a symbol used by a company to identify a product as belonging to its brand. It is usually a small shape, word, or series of letters. Only buy brand name goods if they are the best you can get for the price, not in the hope that a logo will impress someone else.

56 Don't let friends convince you that you can *only* be cool if you buy products of a specific brand. **Peer pressure** should not be the reasoning behind how you spend your money. Base your spending choices on quality and cost, not on conforming to someone else's ideas.

57 Always comparison shop before you buy. This means checking the price on the same or similar items to see where you can get the best deal.

58 Shopping when there are special sales may bag you bargains, but never use sales as an excuse for **impulse buying.**

listen up!

The first thing to get to grips with when budgeting is the difference between *wanting* and *needing*. You may want to download some music or get a new pair of cool boots, but do you really need them? The answer isn't always no! A pair of great boots can still fulfill a need if they don't cost more than they should. One reason for earning and saving money is so you can sometimes afford to get things you want, even if you don't really need them.

Making the most of your money

When you are going shopping, there are many ways you can make your hard-earned cash stretch.

59 Always take advantage of shop loyalty cards or preferred customer points schemes. They can save you money in the long run.

60 Collecting coupons is not just for your granny! There are often coupons in newspapers, magazines, or online that will give discounts or two-for-one deals.

Buying sale items at the end of a season can make your money go much further.

61 Check the labels on clothes, or the packaging of products, to see where the item is made. You can then research the work practices in that country to see if they are fair.

62 Do some internet research for information about the **ethical** work practices of shops and brands. Their websites might have a section explaining how the company tries to be ethical or green.

Make sure the things you buy have been produced ethically and are not damaging to the environment.

 When is a bargain not a bargain?

 When retailers aren't quite telling the whole truth! Trading and advertising standards (laws) prevent retailers from telling outright lies. However, they can still be very sneaky...

- A sale item in one shop may not really have been more expensive there, but only at another shop in the chain.

- Shops will advertise items at very cheap sale prices but there are actually only very small numbers available. They hope that customers will come to get those products and then spend their money on other things when they can't get what they want.

- Another trick is the use of a loss leader. This is when a heavily discounted item is promoted to tempt you into the shop in the hope you will also buy full-price items.

Oops! Beware! Store cards are *not* the same as shop loyalty cards. Store cards are credit cards run by shops, and can be used only to buy products in that shop or at others in the same chain. Using store cards can lead to debts, so avoid them unless there are real benefits.

listen up!

When you spend your money on a burger or a roast beef sandwich, you don't imagine that you are contributing to the destruction of the rainforest – but you might be! For example, the need for cattle grazing land to meet the demands of the beef market has been a major cause of South American rainforest clearance.

63 Look for special logos that identify products as ethically produced or environmentally sound. These include Fairtrade, Organic Cotton, Earth Positive, Fair Wear Foundation, Ethical Junction, and many others.

64 Think about the **carbon footprint** of a product. Is there something made more locally that would be just as good?

What's that?

A **carbon footprint** means the total amount of greenhouse gases emitted by an activity or the making of a product. Your carbon footprint is made up of all of the greenhouse-gas-creating activities that you cause over a given period of time.

case study

Watch out for "not included"!

Erin went to buy a new printer at a large computer discount store. She'd done some research and reckoned she'd found the best deal. Luckily, just before she got to the front of the checkout queue to pay, she noticed, "Ink cartridges not included" written on the box. With the extra cost of the cartridges, it turned out that another printer that included cartridges in the price was actually much cheaper.

Oops!

Most people know about the addictive power of alcohol and drugs, but did you know that shopping can be addictive, too? When a person does something they enjoy, it causes the release of a substance called an endorphin into the bloodstream. Endorphins reinforce the enjoyment. Some people need to feel that pleasure again and again. Others become shopping addicts because of low self-esteem. Shopping addiction can be as difficult to break as an alcohol or drug habit.

Q Are the symptoms of a shopping addiction just high spending?

A No. A true shopping addict buys things he or she doesn't need, or buys ridiculous numbers of the same item. Most items never get used and are hidden away, or even destroyed. Buying stuff gives shopping addicts some temporary relief from the negative feelings they have about life, but it can lead to shame, remorse, and guilt.

true story

Celebrity spending gone mad!

Elton John, Katie Holmes, Mike Tyson, and Britney Spears have all hit the headlines with their spending habits. But the celebrity who has really caught media attention is the former child star, actress Lindsay Lohan. She has been reported to have spent up to £9,500 ($15,000) a week on shopping sprees, and £4,400 ($7,000) a month on her hair!

Fun for (almost) free

Yes! You really can have fun and do interesting things without breaking the bank! New is nice, but new-to-you is almost as good! Swapping things with friends or buying things from second-hand or charity shops can help you keep your money in your pocket, or in the bank.

Old clothes or fabric from a jumble sale can be snipped and sewed into something unique for very little money.

listen up!

Group money saving and earning activities can be fun *and* economical.

65 Get together with a group of friends and choose a swap party theme, for example, clothes, DVDs, CDs, video games, or books.

66 Arrange a "trash into cash" sale of unwanted goods with a group of friends. You can divide the money up or pool it together for a group outing or treat.

67 If you and your friends need new outfits for a special event, make a group decision to get everything you need second-hand or from charity shops. See who can spend the least on great things.

Kate Moss and charity shop chic

Many high-profile celebrities get their super-cool, chic looks from wearing second-hand clothes. Kate Moss has often been spotted trawling through charity shops for some of the individual outfits that keep her at the forefront of style. Since becoming a part-time clothes designer, Kate admits that many of the pieces in her latest collection are based on used items she bought from charity shops in the United Kingdom and the United States.

It's all in the words. If you say "second-hand" or "used" clothes, it sounds … well, tacky! If you say "retro" or "vintage fashion", suddenly it's *uber* cool.

Here are some things to bear in mind when buying second-hand:

68 To get the best value out of second-hand items, avoid over-worn, damaged, or stained clothing.

69 Buy items for their individual parts. For example, great buttons can be cut off a not-so-great shirt and used on something else.

70 Charity shops are great places to get accessories. Look out for funky and original belts, ties, and bags.

71 Look in the bric-a-brac sections of charity shops for original gifts, or for interesting and quirky things to personalize your room.

Short of money? Make it yourself!

Another way to plug the gap in your limited finances is to make things you might want or need, either for yourself or as presents for your family and friends. It's personal, thoughtful, and cheap!

72 Think twice before spending money on manufactured greetings cards. Some are ridiculously expensive for what they are. Instead, attach a small paper label to a gift or lock into your creativity and make the card yourself!

73 Think creatively (and economically) when wrapping gifts. Newspaper tied up with colourful strips of fabric can look great. Or try using old wallpaper offcuts or leftover bits of fabric.

74 Family and friends always appreciate gifts of food. Something tasty and homemade always wins out over shop-bought goods.

75 Consider offering vouchers for your services as gifts. These could be for gardening, cleaning, babysitting, or many other things. Make sure it's something you're really good at, such as painting fingernails or sorting out computer problems.

If you receive a personal, handmade gift, you have something that is one of a kind.

> **"One of the best presents I ever had was an amazing piece of art my cousin made out of junk ... It made my room look like a trendy art gallery."**
>
> Dave

More flash than cash

You want to have a laugh with your friends, but no one can afford to spend the cash? Why not try some do-it-yourself fun! Keeping your money in your pocket doesn't need to be boring.

76 Have a DVD theme night at someone's house. Make a list of all the films you already have on a particular theme – such as horror or science fiction – then vote for the two you want to watch. If everyone chips in for snacks, the cost will be minimal.

77 If the weather is good, explore the great outdoors! A picnic with a Frisbee, even if it's just in a local park, can be a nearly free day out.

78 Go geek and have a Scrabble or other board game competition with your friends. You know you'll enjoy it, especially if someone makes crazy winner and runners-up certificates to hand out at the end.

79 Video arcades eat money! Make a list of all the games you and your friends have, and create a lending system.

Fun with friends does not mean spending loads of cash.

Stuff can get wrecked

One of the simplest ways to be money smart is to look after the possessions you value. Failing to do this is wasting money you've already spent. If you keep your stuff in good condition, you have the option of selling things on for good prices when you don't want them any more.

80 Never put drinks on or near electrical equipment, especially computers. It's not only dangerous, but accidental spillages can cause damage that will cost a lot to repair or replace.

81 Put music CDs and DVDs back in their cases to prevent them getting scratched or cracked.

82 Make sure that bikes and sports equipment are properly stored and maintained to keep them safe and in good working order.

83 Favourite items of clothing will last a lot longer if they are kept clean and don't have to live in piles on the floor. A pair of expensive football boots is more likely to last if properly cleaned after a muddy game.

Looking after expensive possessions, such as bicycles, can save you money in the long term.

Q What is replacement insurance?

A This is insurance you can buy for some expensive items, such as mobile phones and MP3 players. You pay a monthly or yearly **premium** and, depending on the policy, you will be able to get a replacement if the item is lost, stolen, or broken. But if the premiums are high compared to the value of your item, it might not be worth it, and there are many dodgy policies out there. Also, some items may already be covered by your parents' general household insurance.

Sports equipment costs a lot of money. Things like football boots last longer and perform better if you take good care of them.

Mobile phones don't float

Archie and his friends were leaning over the side of a canal footbridge. By the time Archie realized that his mobile phone was slipping out of his top pocket, it was too late to stop it. It sank like a stone. If Archie had been a bit more careful, he wouldn't have had to spend lots of money on a new phone.

Julia's phone mysteriously disappeared one day. Ten days later, her dad saw something strange in the bottom of the toilet bowl. It was the silver tip of the aerial of Julia's mobile phone. It had fallen into the toilet and got jammed in the "u" bend. Julia was lucky because she happened to have a good insurance policy that covered "serious water damage". And the rest – yuck!

Spending and saving online

As well as being a great tool for communicating with friends and researching information, the internet is now at the forefront of retail and banking. But is it a safe and sensible place to spend and save your money?

Online banking is used by millions of people around the world. Even people with normal high street bank accounts can usually check information by accessing their accounts online. It is convenient and can be used 24/7. Online banking is a reality. You just need to make sure you are using it in the safest way.

listen up!

84 Make sure your computer has full and up-to-date virus protection. This will help keep out many virus-based online banking scams, such as **Trojans**.

85 Protect yourself from nasties sneaking into your computer via your broadband connection by installing a **firewall** barrier.

86 Don't fall foul of **phishing**! This type of scam sends out emails that look as if they're from real, well-known companies, or even banks. These try to trick you into giving out your account numbers, passwords, or personal information by saying they need to "update your records". *Remember, no bank or reputable company will ever ask you for that kind of information in an email, or ask you to enter that type of detail at a click-through website.*

87 When your computer alerts you that there's an update or "patch" available for your operating system or your web browser, don't push "Ask me again later"! These updates and patches are the most effective tools against new scams, and have often been specially created to plug the holes in an existing protective system.

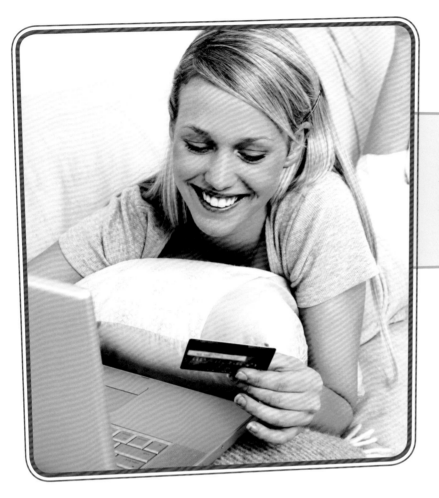

Before you buy online, make sure the site you're using is safe and that the company is trustworthy.

Q What is a computer "patch"?

A A computer patch is like a patch used to repair a hole in a bicycle tyre. When technicians realize that something in the system doesn't work, or could be easily attacked by online scams, they create a small bit of software that can be loaded in to solve the problem. If you don't download and install patches, then your computer is full of holes and can leak your details.

Buying and selling online

Nothing can be more convenient or satisfying than buying or selling items online. It seems like lots of gratification for very little effort - but is it as good as it seems?

88 You may think you're getting a better deal on the internet compared to high street shops, but always remember to factor in the extras. Do you have to pay for postage or delivery? Is the payment method used secure, or will your financial details be at risk?

89 Beware of companies that pop up on the internet offering unbelievably good deals, take your payment, and then mysteriously vanish without supplying the goods. If a price seems unbelievable, DON'T BELIEVE IT.

90 Always check the returns and repair policy before buying something online. It's easy to go into a local shop and negotiate a repair or replacement for faulty goods, but in the cyber world it might not be so simple.

You need to be 18 years old or over to use the online bookseller Amazon and the auction site eBay. Other buying and selling sites have similar rules. If you want to use these sites, you will have to do so with your parents.

listen up!

BE SMART

Using the internet for savvy shopping research

The internet is a great tool for researching good-value products. You can compare features and prices by checking out a variety of possible retailers online. Some retailers will even let you know if the item is available in their shops and allow you to reserve one by using a special feature on their website.

Oops!

You may be very safe and responsible with your cards and PIN number, but is your identity safe online? When something is physically stolen, you usually know it has happened. When your identity is stolen online you may never know until problems occur. So, what can you do to avoid identity theft?

- Always use a password with a combination of letters and numbers that will be difficult for someone else to guess.
- Install browser security software.
- Keep your computer clean! Regularly delete your internet search history, your temporary files, and empty your recycling bin.
- Use a system developed to identify any **cookies** on your computer.

What's that?

In computer language, a **cookie** is a message sent from a web server to your browser when you visit a website. The next time you visit, it knows what you looked at last time. Cookies cannot pass on viruses or access your hard drive, but they can record your usage of a website and any details you pass on to a website.

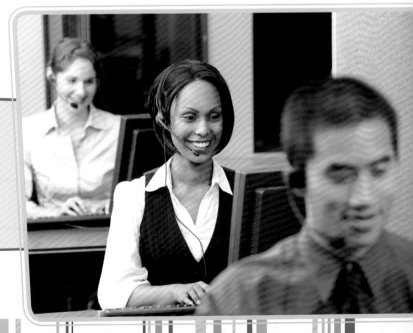

When you buy things over the telephone or online you can never be sure where your details may end up.

Don't break the law to save money

Most of the information on the internet is there to use for free. But some things require payment to use, or are illegal to download and share with others. Don't get caught out, it's not worth it.

Be sure what you are doing is legal.

listen up!

91 Always use a legitimate source when you buy and download music or films. Anywhere that lets you download current chart music or recently released films for free is NOT legitimate.

92 Never justify illegal file-sharing by the fact that it saves you money. Illegal file-sharing is just as much a criminal act as if you took a DVD off a shop shelf, put it in your pocket and walked out. It is theft.

Q What is file-sharing?

A It is the copying and sharing of digital information, such as computer data and multimedia files. Not all file-sharing is illegal, only when it involves **copyright**-protected material.

"[Illegal file-sharing] is just so unfair to new acts trying to make it in the industry."

Lily Allen, singer

Joel Tenenbaum's big fine

In 2009 American student Joel Tenenbaum was taken to court by the Recording Industry Association of America (RIAA) for illegally file-sharing 30 downloaded songs. He was convicted and fined $675,000 (about £400,000). The fine was later reduced to $67,500 (about £42,000), which still comes to $2,250 (about £1,400) per song!

The RIAA has convinced United States courts that large fines are the best way to show people that illegal file-sharing can be a costly mistake. However, some people feel that the big music companies are just trying to protect their profits. Instead, they should be coming up with new ways of working. What do you think?

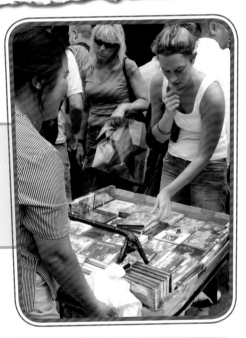

Buying DVDs from a dodgy trader at a street market is taking part in an illegal act. It cheats everyone who helped create the film.

BE SMART

Illegal downloading

Recently released films often make it on to the internet where they can be downloaded for free or for a small fee. This is illegal. The only way a new film gets on the internet is if a legitimate copy of the film has been stolen and reproduced online, or if someone has illegally gone into a cinema and filmed it during a performance. The sound and visual quality of a copied film is usually rubbish.

Scams and pitfalls

When you start to look at all the problems, it seems that few things can be as dangerous or difficult as holding on to your money, or spending it safely. There are definitely scammers out there. But by being money smart and knowing what to look for, you can keep on the right track.

"A fool and his money are soon parted."

Thomas Tusser, 16th-century English writer

Money scams: the same old same old

Many types of money scams have been around for hundreds of years and only the details have changed. For example, 200 years ago, a travelling "professor" or "doctor" might have tried to sell you an anti-ageing potion off the back of a horse and cart. A hundred years ago, the same useless product might have been advertised in a magazine or newspaper. Thirty years ago, you would have received junk mail, or perhaps a telephone call advertising a similar product. These days, it's more likely to turn up on the internet. But it's the same old scam! Here are a few to look out for:

93 Avoid schemes that ask you to pay in advance for products or services. They may never materialize or you may be getting and paying for more than you intended. This is the case with mobile phone ringtone purchase scams. You think you are paying a one-off fee to buy ringtones, but find that you have entered into an agreement where money is being debited monthly from your bank account.

94 One major group of scams tells you that you have won a prize draw or a competition and need to pay a delivery fee or tax. Some of these scams ask for personal information or your bank details to "verify" your entry. Never give this information away. It is the first step to full identity theft.

95 Beware of bogus charities! They can target you door-to-door, by letter, by telephone, or on the street. All official charities are registered and most have well-known names, either nationally or in your local area.

96 Think twice before you dial! High-cost phone lines are now the norm for phone-in competitions and computer helplines, amongst others. When you call one of these lines, and then wait and wait (and wait and wait) for help, you are being charged at the highest rate the whole time.

97 Watch out when using ATM machines! In one scam, a device is inserted into the card slot and records the information to clone the card. Another scam uses a small camera, sometimes in a mobile phone, to photograph the customer entering the PIN. Never use an ATM machine that looks like it has been tampered with, and always cover the keypad with your other hand when entering your PIN.

When you are using an ATM, always check carefully that no one has tampered with the machine. Look out for anything stuck on to the card slot area or in the overhang above the machine.

Q What does *caveat emptor* mean?

A *Caveat emptor* means "let the buyer beware" in Latin. It is the responsibility of a buyer or user of a service to be sure that the product he or she is getting is what was expected. If you buy a cheap, synthetic jumper, you can't expect it to be as high quality as a similar jumper made of 100 per cent wool.

In most countries, consumers are protected by laws. You can return faulty products or cancel contracts for goods or services within a certain period of time.

case study

Teen dream almost turns to nightmare

Have you ever dreamt of making it as a singer, actor, or model? Watch out, there are cheats and scammers out there waiting to take advantage of those dreams.

Thirteen-year-old Pippa and her friends were approached at a big fashion show by a man and woman who claimed to be scouts from a major model agency. They said Pippa's tall and quirky look was just what the agency wanted.

Pippa was flattered, but not stupid. She talked it over with her mum and sister. This so-called agency wanted her to pay a registration fee, plus more money for photographs and training. Pippa soon realized that, rather than being her big break, it was probably a scam. She decided not to take the offer any further.

Pippa's experience is not unique. Trading Standards Offices get many reports of teen model agency scams. They recommend that wannabe models only approach legitimate agencies, like those who are members of the Association of Model Agents, or get advice from websites such as www.safemodelling.org.uk.

Oops!

Not all money scams come from outsiders trying to cheat you. Sometimes you can be your own worst enemy!

Today, more than ever, gambling is everywhere – and it can be the quickest way to lose your money! From fruit machines to lotteries to online poker, everyone wants to convince you to part with your money in the hope of winning big. However, there are always more losers than winners, and in some forms of gambling (such as national lotteries) the odds are millions to one against you ever winning a single penny.

Like drug addicts and alcoholics, some people become addicted to gambling. One small win makes them hope they may keep winning. The best way to stop yourself getting caught up in such a destructive and expensive cycle is to avoid gambling altogether.

If you think you have an addiction, get help from a recognized help group such as Gamblers Anonymous.

Why do we need money?

Why do we bother with money? Couldn't we get on just as well trading one thing for another? Banks, cards, cash, people out to cheat you, sometimes it all seems just a bit much! But it's also too late to go back now. Human beings have been using money in one form or another for at least 2,700 years.

Today, the value is not in the money itself, as it was with gold, silver, and copper coins in the past. Instead its value is set by national governments and agencies such as the World Bank and International Monetary Fund.

Metal coins have been used to pay for things since ancient times.

Oops!

Trading and bartering was fine when you could do it with people you knew in a limited area, and could work out the value of apples as compared to potatoes. But could we still do that now? Could you buy a computer with potatoes, or offer your skills as a doctor for apples? What if you had particularly healthy patients? You could get very hungry!

98 Find out if any local companies are quoted on the **stock market** and follow how they are doing by looking at the stock market reports in newspapers or online. It helps you to understand how your local economy is doing and how it fits in with national and international economic trends.

What's that?

A **stock market** is a place where organized trading of company **shares** takes place. Shares are individual bits of ownership – a "share" of the company. Each share has a value that can go up or down depending on the popularity of the company. Many countries have a national stock market.

99 Learn more about **investment**. If buying stocks for real seems too scary, set up a fantasy stocks and **shares** game between you and some friends. Start out with the same pretend amount of investment money and use it to "buy" a group of different stocks. Follow how the stocks do over a set period and see whose investments come out on top. It's all of the fun with none of the fear.

listen up!

Every time you buy something like a DVD or a magazine, or deposit money in your bank account, you are taking part in the international monetary system. The money you spend and save becomes part of the workings of local and national **financial institutions** that then interact with others around the globe. Like you and your friends, money doesn't stay in one place any more. It is invested and spent all over the world.

Financing your future

It's no good to suddenly think when you turn 18 that it would be a great idea to take a year off to travel around the world before starting university or getting a job. You'll need the cash to finance your dreams. When your savings are making money for you through interest payments, you can start planning for future spending!

By saving up over time, you are more likely to be able to afford to live an exciting and adventurous life.

100 Don't be a money ostrich! To hide your head in the sand and pretend that money and family finances are something you don't have to worry about is immature and hard on your parents. Talk about money issues with your family and there are less likely to be unpleasant surprises or unreal expectations.

Q What is deferred gratification?

A This is temporarily putting off something you really want to do or have in order to wait for something that might give you greater pleasure. Going out to buy a film released on DVD today is instant gratification. Saving up for three years to buy a car is deferred gratification.

case study

Daniel wanted to learn to fly a plane practically from the moment he knew what a plane was. Before he was 10 years old he was already saving up for flying lessons. He always asked for cash for birthdays and Hanukkah, and got a Saturday job as soon as he was able, with most of his cash going into the flying fund.

When he finally started flying lessons, they lived up to his expectations. Dan did his solo flight and got his pilot's licence before learning to drive! He is now at university studying aeronautic engineering, and he's still flying.

Money is not great in itself – it is just a way to buy stuff. You need some of that stuff to survive, such as food, clothing, and shelter. Other things make your life nicer or make you more comfortable. But wealth is not the answer to all of life's problems. Money will not tell you how to make good friends, or what music to like, or what subject to study at university. Large amounts of money can sometimes even make your life more difficult, with more responsibilities and more challenging choices.

listen up!

101 Always see money and wealth in perspective. Understand what money can and can't do. As the old saying goes, "money can't buy you happiness".

Glossary

accountant someone who is professionally trained to a high level to deal with the finances of organizations and individuals

carbon footprint total of the emission of greenhouse gases caused by an activity or the production of a product. A person's carbon footprint is the sum of all of the greenhouse gas-creating activities that he or she caused to occur over a given period of time.

clone term used by banks to describe credit or debit cards that have had their details copied and used illegally

cookie message sent from a web server to a person's web browser identifying information a person is using or entering on to a website

copyright law that protects the right to use and ownership of musical, artistic, and literary works. Copyright law gives the creator of a work the exclusive ownership of their creation for a set period of time.

counterfeit make an exact imitation of something, such as money, in order to deceive people

credit history record of all borrowings and repayments made by a person

curriculum vitae Latin for the "course of life". It is used to describe a brief report of a person's education and work experience as well as certain biographical details. It is usually used to support an application for a job, or for education or training. The initials CV are often used as a short form.

entrepreneur someone who starts or organizes a business, usually taking a financial risk

ethical goods that are produced and sold in ways that are fair to the people who have worked on them

financial institution organization such as a bank or building society

financial literacy understanding of money and finances

firewall system installed in a personal computer or in a computer network to block unauthorized access and usage, but allow authorized access and usage

fraudulent usage illegal use of something with an intention to deceive

impulse buying purchasing an item without much care or thought. Impulse buys are often not needed or are poor value for the money spent.

interest amount of money paid on savings or charged on borrowings or debt. The interest rate is the percentage paid or charged.

investment using money to make a profit

mortgage loan taken out to buy property

peer pressure pressure from your friends or others in a similar age group to influence how you act or what you think

phishing email scam where the scammer tries to get information from you by making you think you are dealing with a real, legitimate company. Some forms of phishing are also known as "spoofing".

premium amount paid by a policyholder for coverage under an insurance contract

share small unit of ownership of a company

stock market place where shares are bought and sold. Some countries have national stock markets.

Trojan computer program that seems to be useful but is designed to be harmful. Trojans can destroy information on your computer.

Find out more

Books

Life Skills: Managing Money, Barbara Hollander (Heinemann Library, 2009)

Life Skills: Raising Money, Barbara Hollander (Heinemann Library, 2009)

Show Me the Money, Alvin Hall (Dorling Kindersley, 2008)

Smart Saving Tips, Jane Furnival (Hay House, 2007)

The Spend Less Handbook: 365 Tips for a Better Quality of Life While Actually Spending Less, Rebecca Ash (Harriman House, 2006)

Websites

www.pfeg.org
This is the website of a charitable trust, the Personal Finance Education Group. It contains loads of advice and information divided into three age ranges: 4-11 years, 12-16 years, and 16-19 years.

www.banksafeonline.co.uk
This is the website of the banking industry organization that gives advice about banking online and how to keep your money safe.

www.safemodelling.co.uk
This website is run by the Institute of Modelling to provide a free information resource on how to stay safe in the world of modelling.

www.ethicalconsumer.org/FreeBuyersGuides/clothing.aspx
This website has lots of information about ethical shopping.

www.moneyadvicetrust.org
This is the website of a charity that was set up to help people with debt problems. It also collects and archives news items dealing with debt and other money problems.

www.citizensadvice.org.uk
This is the website of the Citizens Advice Bureau. This organization offers all kinds of advice, including money help on its website and in its high street offices.

Topics to research

- Can using the internet help you save money? Price up an item you are interested in buying using brand websites and price comparison websites. Work out how you can get the best bargains. Remember to be careful if you are considering buying online.

- Does budgeting save you money? Try making yourself a budget for a week or a month. Work out which expenditures are the most important. If you can, factor in earning and saving to your budget.

- Find out more about music copyright law and the problem of illegal downloading. Are you and your friends getting your music legally? What are governments and the music industry doing to tackle the problem of illegal downloads and file sharing?

- Play a fantasy stock market game with your friends or classmates. Each of you could begin with the same budget and then research the best shares to "buy" and when to "sell". See who comes out on top after a few months as a fantasy investor.

Index